The
LITTLE
SAIL BOAT
By LOIS LENSKI

HENRY Z. WALCK, INC.
NEW YORK

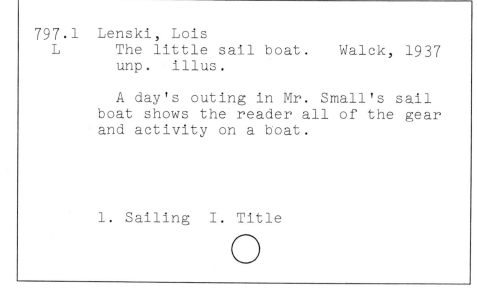

797.1 Lenski, Lois
  L   The little sail boat.   Walck, 1937
         unp. illus.

         A day's outing in Mr. Small's sail
      boat shows the reader all of the gear
      and activity on a boat.

         1. Sailing I. Title

This Main Entry catalog card may be reproduced without permission

The Little Sail-Boat

Captain Small has a sail-boat. He keeps it anchored off-shore.

It is a fine day. Captain Small gets into his row-boat and rows out. He is taking his fishing-line, lunch basket and small dog, Tinker, with him.

Captain Small takes
in the oars and makes
the row-boat fast to
the mooring.

He gets aboard
the sail-boat and hoists
the sail.

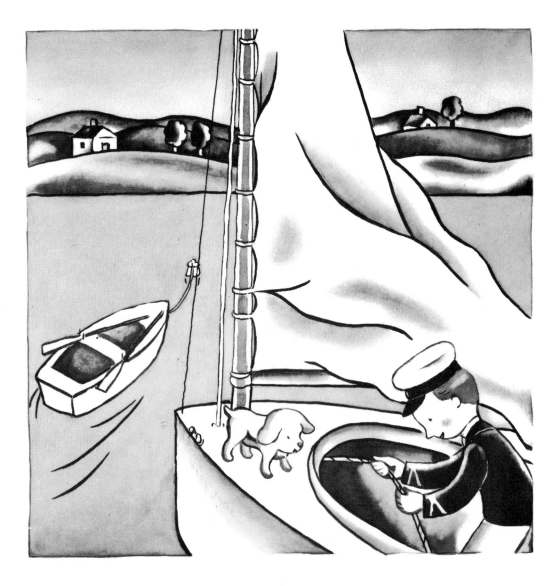

He drops the mooring and the boat starts to move. Tinker sits in the bow. He likes to sail, too.

Sitting in the stern, Captain Small takes the tiller and puts the boat before the wind. He sails for some distance.

He decides to jibe ~ to turn toward the shore. He pulls the tiller and ducks his head to let the sail swing over to the other side.

Now he is sitting with his back to the wind,- or, to windward.

He comes into a quiet little cove where the fishing is good.   He drops the anchor and lowers sail.

Captain Small gets out
his fishing-line and puts
bait on the hook. He throws
it away from the boat; the
cork floats on the water.
Now he is waiting for a
nibble!

He waits...and waits...
but all the fish seem to
be somewhere else. The
sun is hot...and Captain
Small grows tired of
waiting. He falls asleep...

Suddenly a sharp tug on the line wakes him up. He pulls it in and finds a big, fat fish wiggling on the hook. He is so excited that...

He tumbles overboard!
Tinker barks! But never
mind! The water is so
nice and cool, he decides
to enjoy a good swim.

When he climbs back on deck, he feels very hungry, so he and Tinker eat their lunch. The sun soon dries his clothes.

Captain Small rests
awhile and then it is time
to start for home.   He
hoists the sail and raises
anchor.

On the way back, he
sails against the wind
in a zigzag course.

A speed-boat roars by. The waves rock the sail-boat and make the sails flap. Tinker does not like it.

The sky grows dark. The waves splash over the bow. The wind blows hard. The boat heels over and almost upsets. But brave Captain Small brings it up into the wind. Then he sails safely into the bay.

Captain Small makes
the sail-boat fast to the
mooring. He and Tinker get
into the row-boat. He rows
as fast as he can to the dock.

Just as they climb out,
the downpour comes. They
are waiting in the boat-
house until it is over.

After the storm,
Captain Small and Tinker
drive home in
    the little Auto!

That night, Captain Small has fish for supper. Tinker has two dog biscuits.
Are they good ?

Oh my !

Yes,
that's all!